EXPLORING
AMERICA'S REGIONS

EXPLORING
NEW ENGLAND

BY SAMANTHA S. BELL

CONTENT CONSULTANT
Adam Sweeting, PhD
Division of Humanities Chair
Boston University

Core Library

An Imprint of Abdo Publishing
abdopublishing.com

Cover image: The Portland Head Light is the oldest
lighthouse in Maine.

abdopublishing.com

Published by Abdo Publishing, a division of ABDO, PO Box 398166, Minneapolis, Minnesota 55439. Copyright © 2018 by Abdo Consulting Group, Inc. International copyrights reserved in all countries. No part of this book may be reproduced in any form without written permission from the publisher. Core Library™ is a trademark and logo of Abdo Publishing.

Printed in the United States of America, North Mankato, Minnesota
102017
012018

Cover Photo: E. J. Johnson Photography/Shutterstock Images
Interior Photos: E. J. Johnson Photography/Shutterstock Images, 1; Stuart Monk/Shutterstock Images, 4–5, 45; Red Line Editorial, 7, 28; Debra Millet/Shutterstock Images, 8; North Wind Picture Archives, 10–11; Randy Duchaine/Alamy, 16; Shutterstock Images, 18–19, 24–25, 43; Donald Gargano/Shutterstock Images, 21; Joe Raedle/Getty Images News/Getty Images, 30–31; M. Chebby/iStockphoto, 32; Scott Eisen/Getty Images News/Getty Images, 36–37

Editor: Megan Ellis
Imprint Designer: Maggie Villaume
Series Design Direction: Ryan Gale

Publisher's Cataloging-in-Publication Data

Names: Bell, Samantha S., author.
Title: Exploring New England / by Samantha S. Bell.
Description: Minneapolis, Minnesota : Abdo Publishing, 2018. | Series: Exploring America's regions | Includes online resources and index.
Identifiers: LCCN 2017946942 | ISBN 9781532113802 (lib.bdg.) | ISBN 9781532152689 (ebook)
Subjects: LCSH: Atlantic Coast (New England)--Juvenile literature. | Discovery and exploration--Juvenile literature. | Travel--Juvenile literature. | United States--Historical geography--Juvenile literature.
Classification: DDC 917.40--dc23
LC record available at https://lccn.loc.gov/2017946942

CONTENTS

WELCOME TO NEW ENGLAND

New England is a region of beautiful scenery. Waterfalls flow down the mountainsides. Colorful fall trees line the roadways. Sandy beaches range for miles and miles. It's no wonder that New England attracts so many people.

New England is in the northeastern United States. It includes the states of Maine, Vermont, New Hampshire, Massachusetts, Rhode Island, and Connecticut.

New England is known for its covered bridges, which span many of the region's rivers.

SIZE

New England is approximately 72,000 square miles (186,500 sq km) in area. Rhode Island is the smallest state in New England. It is also the smallest state in the United States. It covers 1,545 square miles (4,002 sq km). The largest state in New England is Maine. It covers 35,385 square miles (91,646 sq km).

Vermont has the smallest population in New England. Approximately 600,000 people live in Vermont. Almost 7 million people live in Massachusetts. Boston, Massachusetts,

FALL COLORS

New England is known for its fall leaves. The colors depend on the soil, the weather, and the altitude. The types of trees also play a role. Pine trees do not change color at all. Red maple leaves turn red. Leaves from dogwood trees turn purple and gold. Every year, thousands of people visit New England to see the fall leaves. In late September, the leaves are most vibrant in Maine, Vermont, and New Hampshire. By mid-October, the colors can be seen in Connecticut, Massachusetts, and Rhode Island.

MAP OF
NEW ENGLAND

This map shows the states in New England. Note the lakes and mountains in the region. Based on the geography of New England, what do you think some of the region's important industries might be?

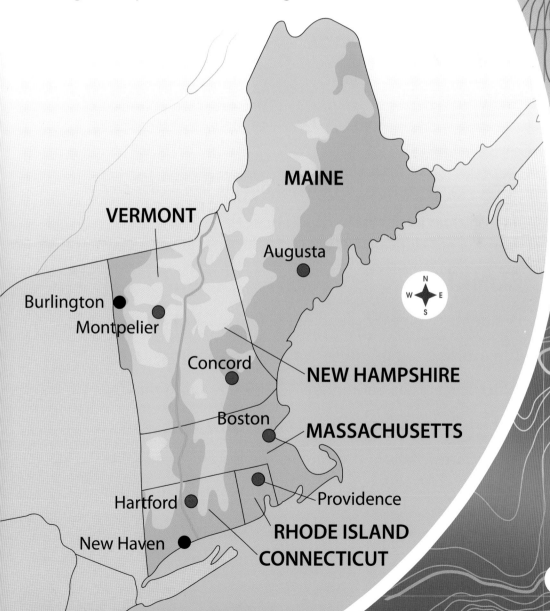

MAINE

VERMONT

Augusta

Burlington
Montpelier

Concord

NEW HAMPSHIRE

Boston

MASSACHUSETTS

Hartford

Providence

New Haven

RHODE ISLAND
CONNECTICUT

Summer is a popular season to explore Lake Champlain by boat.

is the region's largest city. More people live in the city of Boston than in the state of Vermont.

CLIMATE

Residents of New England enjoy four distinct seasons. The average temperature in summer is approximately 80 to 85 degrees Fahrenheit (26–29°C) during the day. In the fall, some leaves turn bright red, orange, and yellow. Snow falls in the winter. Temperatures can drop to 25 degrees Fahrenheit (-3°C) during the day. In the spring, buds appear on the trees and flowers bloom.

GEOGRAPHY

New England has beaches, lakes, hills, and mountains. All of the states except Vermont have beaches on the Atlantic Ocean. Lake Champlain in Vermont is the largest lake in the region. Mountain ranges include the White Mountains in New Hampshire and Maine, and the Green Mountains in Vermont. These mountains are part of the larger Appalachian Mountain range.

PERSPECTIVES
HIGH ADVENTURE

Mount Washington in New Hampshire is the tallest mountain in New England. It is also a favorite destination for ice climbers. Every year, thousands of people climb Mount Washington. It is not easy. Temperatures drop to -30 degrees F (-34°C) in the winter. Strong winds make it dangerous. But the excitement keeps the climbers coming back again and again. As climber Mark Synnot explains, "Somewhere deep inside every ice climber is a barbarian who craves hard work and sticky situations where survival can't be taken for granted."

RICH IN HISTORY

Native Americans first settled the New England region. The Eastern Algonquian tribes shared similar languages and cultures. They included the Abenaki in Maine, the Mohegans in Connecticut, and the Wampanoag in Massachusetts. Trails and waterways connected the tribes for trade.

When Europeans came to the region, they traded with the Native Americans too. By 1600, they arrived from France, England, and the Netherlands. They exchanged metal, glass, and cloth for beaver pelts.

Wampanoag leader Massasoit made a treaty with the Pilgrims in Massachusetts.

The Europeans unknowingly brought new diseases with them. In some areas, up to 90 percent of the Native American population died from disease.

In 1614, an English explorer named John Smith came to the region. He named it New England.

EUROPEAN SETTLERS

The first permanent European settlers arrived in November 1620. Many wanted religious freedom from the Church of England. They were known as Pilgrims. They established the Plymouth Colony in Massachusetts. But they were not prepared for the harsh winter. Many died of cold and hunger.

A Pawtuxet tribe member named Squanto helped the Pilgrims. Squanto lived with the Wampanoag and their chief, Massasoit. He taught the Pilgrims how to fish and plant crops. Massasoit made a peaceful alliance with the Pilgrims.

More English colonists settled in New Hampshire, Connecticut, and Rhode Island. Many came because they wanted a new start.

In 1638, Europeans started bringing enslaved people from Africa and the West Indies. New England merchants owned many of the slave ships. During the 1700s, Newport, Rhode Island, controlled between 60 and 90 percent of the slave trade in the North American colonies.

As their towns grew, colonists demanded more land from the Native American tribes. In 1675, tribes came together under the Pokunoket chief known

THE FIRST COLLEGE

Harvard University is in Cambridge, Massachusetts. Established in 1636, it is the oldest college in the United States. It was named after a young minister in New England named John Harvard. He gave 400 books and half of his estate to the college. The first graduation ceremony was held in 1642. There were nine graduates.

as King Philip. They fought to drive out the colonists. Approximately 2,500 colonists and 5,000 Native Americans died. Some Native Americans escaped to Canada. Many were sold into slavery.

COLONIES TO COUNTRY

The colonies were under English rule until the 1770s. But many colonists wanted independence. Boston became the center of the American Revolution (1775–1783). Those who opposed English rule gathered to protest English taxes, such as the tax on tea. In 1773, a group boarded three English ships in Boston Harbor. They threw 342 chests of tea into the water. Known as the Boston Tea Party, this action pushed the two sides closer to war.

The first battle of the American Revolution took place in Lexington, Massachusetts, in 1775. The war lasted eight long years. The colonists won, and the United States was a free country. After the war, states in New England gradually outlawed slavery.

FARMS TO FACTORIES

In 1790, Samuel Slater built a textile mill on the Blackstone River in Rhode Island. It was one of the first factories in the United States. By the mid-1800s, there were more than 100 textile mills in Rhode Island. More were established throughout New England. Thousands of people worked in the mills. Manufacturing replaced farming as the main industry.

The Slater Mill in Pawtucket, Rhode Island, was one of the first cotton-spinning factories in the United States. In 1925, it became a museum.

Mills brought jobs and wealth to New England. But during the Great Depression in the 1930s, many mills were forced to shut down. People lost their jobs. The factories were used again during World War II (1939–1945). Factories in Waterbury, Connecticut, produced food, clothing, shelter, ammunition, and equipment for the soldiers. They were open all day and all night.

STRAIGHT TO THE
SOURCE

In 1894, Josephine St. Pierre Ruffin founded the Women's New Era Club for black women in Boston. She organized the First National Conference of Colored Women in 1895. The goals of the conference were to discuss civil rights issues of the day, find inspiration in other members, and advance the lives of black women. In a speech to those attending the conference, Ruffin discussed the importance of black women taking leadership roles:

> [I]t is especially fitting that the women of the race take the lead in this movement, but for all this we recognize the necessity of the sympathy of our husbands, brothers and fathers. Our women's movement is woman's movement in that it is led and directed by women for the good of women and men, for the benefit of all humanity, which is more than any one branch or section of it . . . If there is any one thing I would especially enjoin upon this conference it is union and earnestness.

> Source: Josephine St. Pierre Ruffin. "Address to the First National Conference of Colored Women," 1895. Web. Accessed September 25, 2017.

Consider Your Audience
Write a description of Ruffin's address for a younger friend or sibling. How does it differ from the original text? Why?

PLACES TO SEE

New England is a region of beautiful landscapes. Landmarks made by humans and by nature can be found in the towns, along the coast, and in the wilderness.

MAN-MADE LANDMARKS

The Freedom Trail is a 2.5-mile (4-km) route in Boston. Visitors can see 16 historical sites that played a part in the American Revolution. The trail begins at Boston Common, where 1,000 British soldiers camped in 1775. Other sites on the Freedom Trail include the Massachusetts State House and the Paul Revere House.

The statue of George Washington is a popular attraction for people visiting Boston Common.

Mystic Seaport, a museum in Mystic, Connecticut, recreates an important shipbuilding site from the 1800s. It covers 17 square acres (6.9 sq ha). The museum includes more than 60 historic buildings and almost 500 ships. Workers demonstrate the traditional crafts of the 1800s, such as blacksmithing and boat building.

The Cape Neddick Lighthouse sits on a rocky outcrop in York Beach, Maine. It began operating in 1879. The lighthouse stands 41 feet (12.5 m) high.

TWO IMPORTANT LANTERNS

The Old North Church is part of the Freedom Trail in Boston. It is Boston's most visited historical site. The church played a role in the American Revolution. In April 1775, two church members climbed the steeple. Then they held up two lanterns. The lanterns were a signal to the colonists that the British troops were coming by sea. The church is still used today for Sunday services.

The *Charles W. Morgan* is the last wooden whaling ship still afloat in the United States. It is a popular exhibit at Mystic Seaport.

The lighthouse's red light flashes every six seconds. Ship captains can see the light from 13 nautical miles (24 km) away. Approximately 100,000 people travel to see the lighthouse every summer. The Cape Neddick Lighthouse is one of the most photographed lighthouses in the world.

NATURAL LANDMARKS

New England also has many natural landmarks. Kent Falls is a series of waterfalls in Kent, Connecticut. The water cascades into the Housatonic River. The largest waterfall drops approximately 70 feet (21 m). The flow is usually the greatest in the spring when the winter snow melts.

Mohegan Bluffs are on Block Island, Rhode Island. The island is 12 miles (19 km) south of the mainland. These bluffs are made of clay and rise 200 feet (61 m) above the water. Visitors can enjoy the view or take 141 steps down to the beach to swim or surf.

Acadia National Park in Maine is on Mount Desert Island. The island is approximately 108 square miles (280 sq km) in area. Approximately 2 million people visit the island every year. Some drive along the rocky coastline and look at the scenery. Others go swimming, fishing, or boating in the ponds and lakes. Ferries carry them to different parts of the island.

LIFE IN THE WILDERNESS

New England includes many wild places. Some are in the mountains. Others are near the water. All of them are home to a variety of wildlife.

PLANTS

Sugar maple trees are found throughout New England. They grow best in cool, wet climates. In the early spring, they are tapped for sap. The sap is boiled to make maple syrup.

The white birch tree is the state tree of New Hampshire. It is also called the paper birch because its trunk is covered in peeling

Sap is collected from a maple tree by drilling a hole into its trunk.

RETURN OF THE AMERICAN CHESTNUT

Before 1900, American chestnut trees provided food and lumber for people in the eastern United States. But in the early 1900s, trees were brought to the United States from China and Japan. They carried a deadly fungus called chestnut blight. It almost wiped out the American chestnut trees. But some people are trying to bring back the trees. In Maine, volunteers from the American Chestnut Foundation have already planted 27,000 trees across the state. Glen Rea, member of the Maine chapter of the American Chestnut Foundation, explains: "People just love the chestnut tree so much . . . 100 years down the road, it's going to be just a different environment."

white bark. People used to write on the thin strips of bark. White birch trees can live 60 to 80 years. The wood is used to make furniture, window sills, and drumsticks.

Purple fringed bog orchids are wildflowers that grow in wet areas around New England. They can be found in bogs, swamps, and along stream banks. The flowers may be pink, purple, magenta, or white. Large orchids bloom from early summer to midsummer. Smaller ones bloom from midsummer to late summer.

ANIMALS

Moose live in most of New England. They are the largest of all the deer species. They can reach up to six feet (1.8 m) tall at the shoulder and weigh up to 1,000 pounds (454 kg). Moose are so tall that they prefer to eat high grasses and shrubs. They also feed on water plants in ponds and lakes.

Another New England herbivore is the North American porcupine. Porcupines live in forests. They eat leaves, twigs, and

THE COYWOLF

By the 1800s, most of the wolves in New England had either been killed or driven away. Some of the remaining wolves bred with coyotes from the West. The result was the coywolf. Coywolves weigh approximately 40 pounds (18 kg). They have long legs and bushy tails. They hunt in forests and open areas. Coywolves adapt to living in areas with many people. Today, coywolves live throughout New England.

MOOSE DECLINE

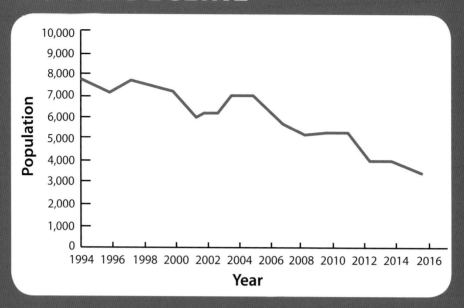

In the last 20 years, the moose population in New Hampshire has decreased by more than 50 percent. Biologists believe this is due to a tick infestation, which occurs when winter temperatures are too warm. What does the graph tell you about the moose decline? What might that mean about the climate in New England?

green plants. Their fur is black to yellow-brown in color. They have hairs with barbs on the ends called quills. A porcupine can have more than 30,000 quills. The quills lie flat until the porcupine is threatened. Then, they stand up to make the attacker leave.

Smooth greensnakes live in the fields, pastures, and meadows of New England. Like their name suggests, these snakes are smooth and green. They are thin, with white or yellow bellies. They are not aggressive. If threatened, smooth greensnakes will slither away, freeze, or sway to imitate a plant in the breeze. In New England, smooth greensnakes hibernate before October. They spend the winter in rock crevices or burrows, coming out again in April or May.

EXPLORE ONLINE

Chapter Four talks about the moose in New England. The article on the website below discusses spotting moose in New Hampshire. As you know, every source is different. What information on the website is the same as the information in Chapter Four? What information is different? What new information did you learn from the website?

WILDLIFE IN NEW HAMPSHIRE: MOOSE

abdocorelibrary.com/exploring-new-england

LARGE AND SMALL BUSINESSES

New England's industries have changed through the years. For example, some factories produce plastics and technology instead of textiles. But some industries, such as commercial fishing and education, have remained.

GOOD FOR BUSINESS

Education is an important industry in New England. The region has many colleges and universities. They include Yale University, the Massachusetts Institute of Technology (MIT),

The Ray and Maria Stata Center at the Massachusetts Institute of Technology (MIT) was designed by famous architect Frank Gehry.

Colorful bands prevent lobsters from opening their claws.

Brown University, and Dartmouth College. Universities in New England have provided new ideas and technology to local businesses. They have also created new jobs for New England residents. In 2000, an MIT graduate started a company in Boston that allows people to share cars. This helps cut down on traffic and pollution.

Tourism is one of New England's largest industries. New England attracts millions of visitors each year. Visitors spend approximately $3 billion during the fall leaf season alone. People come from around the world to experience the region's small towns and historic cities. Some visitors prefer the outdoors. New England has mountain ranges for skiing and lakes for swimming or fishing.

NATURAL RESOURCES

Commercial fishing has been a major part of New England's economy since the 1600s. For hundreds of years, fishers have caught

A BIG CATCH

Lobsters have been part of Maine's coastal economy for a long time. Fishers drop lobster traps down to the ocean floor. A buoy marks their location. Depending on the season, fishers may haul in their traps once a day, once every few days, or once a week. Sometimes the traps have no lobsters. Other times they have as many as 12 in one trap. In 2015, fishers caught more than 120 million pounds (54 million kg) of lobster.

THE OLD WAY

Horse loggers cut each tree individually. A team of horses pulls the logs from the forest. This takes longer than using machines. But horse loggers believe that it is right for the future. Machine operators cut down every tree in a forest. Horse loggers choose old or diseased trees. The good trees are allowed to grow stronger. John Plowden, a horse logger in Maine, says: "What we leave behind, how we treat the woods . . . is worth more than just the money the mill will give you."

bottom-dwelling fish, such as cod and flounder. Recently, the industry has changed. Some species have been overfished. Others have moved away. Instead of cod, some fishers now catch lobster, sea bass, and Maryland blue crab.

Since the 1880s, logging has been a major industry in New Hampshire, Vermont, and Maine. Logging involves cutting down trees to sell as timber or pulp. People make furniture and houses from the timber. They make paper from the pulp. Most of New England's forests have been logged at least once. The largest and most valuable trees are removed. Some loggers clear the land completely. Others take more care with the environment.

Farms in New England produce many types of foods, such as dairy, berries, and maple syrup. Vermont produces the most maple syrup in the United States. Maine is the largest producer of wild blueberries in the world. Blueberry bushes cover 44,000 acres (17,806 ha) in the state.

FURTHER EVIDENCE

Chapter Five contains information about tourism in the New England region. Identify one of the chapter's main points about tourism. What evidence supports this point? The website below, Discover New England, is the region's official tourism organization. Does the information on the website support the main point of the chapter? Does it present new evidence?

DISCOVER NEW ENGLAND

abdocorelibrary.com/exploring-new-england

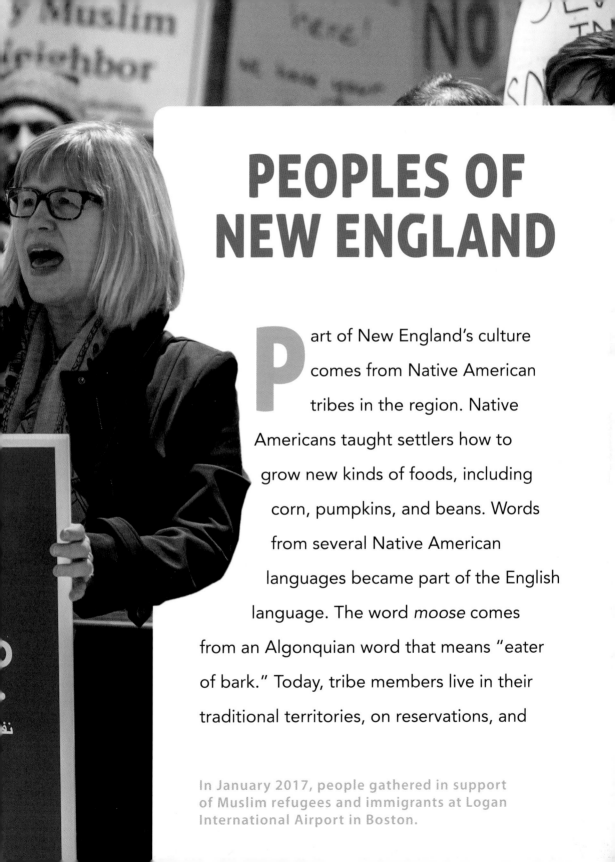

PEOPLES OF NEW ENGLAND

Part of New England's culture comes from Native American tribes in the region. Native Americans taught settlers how to grow new kinds of foods, including corn, pumpkins, and beans. Words from several Native American languages became part of the English language. The word *moose* comes from an Algonquian word that means "eater of bark." Today, tribe members live in their traditional territories, on reservations, and

In January 2017, people gathered in support of Muslim refugees and immigrants at Logan International Airport in Boston.

in other places. They come from such groups as the Eastern Pequot Nation, the Maliseet, the Wampanoag, and the Narragansett.

Immigrants also influence life in New England. In the 1800s and 1900s, more than 1 million people from Ireland and 4 million people from Italy emigrated to New England. Other immigrants during this time included French Canadians, Greeks, and Russian Jews.

FEAST OF THE BLESSED SACRAMENT

Almost 3 percent of New England's population is Portuguese. For more than 100 years, they have been celebrating the Feast of the Blessed Sacrament. It is the largest Portuguese celebration in the world. There is a Sunday mass, a parade, and folk dancing. People eat traditional foods, such as codfish cakes and stewed rabbit.

In recent years, immigrants to New England have come from all over the world. By 2000, there were more than 1 million Latin American residents in New England. Many people also came from China, India, and Vietnam.

Although there isn't a large African-American population in northern New England, African Americans make up approximately 12 percent of the people of Connecticut. They make up approximately 9 percent of the people of Massachusetts.

THE CULTURE OF NEW ENGLAND

New Englanders share some favorite foods. Lobster rolls are made with pieces of lobster meat tucked into a bun. People in Maine eat them cold with mayonnaise. People in Connecticut eat them hot with butter. Cranberries are made into juice, jellies, and pies. Cranberry chutney is a sauce made using cranberries and vinegar.

The arts are found in every New England state. In Connecticut, the Yale University Art Gallery holds a collection of more than 185,000 objects. The gallery first opened in 1832. It is the oldest university art museum in the United States. In Massachusetts, the Boston Ballet Company has been performing for more than 50 years. It includes 70 dancers of 17 different nationalities.

New England also has sporting events. Many of New England's professional sports teams are located in or near Boston. These include football's New England Patriots and baseball's Boston Red Sox. Boston also has the oldest annual marathon. The first race was held in 1897. Today, thousands of people race from all over the world.

The six New England states offer unique experiences for both visitors and residents. It is no wonder it is a favorite destination for so many people.

PERSPECTIVES
RISING TO THE TOP

Mikko Nissinen took over the Boston Ballet in 2001. He made the classes more difficult than ever before. Nissinen believed that being strong helped prevent injuries. The Boston Ballet's programs feature classical dances as well as modern ones. These changes have helped make the Boston Ballet company one of the best in the country. Nissinen views ballet as something that is alive and changing. He sees ballet "not as a museum or church but as living theatre."

STRAIGHT TO THE
SOURCE

Mel Allen is a writer for *New England Today*. Here he considers what draws people to New England:

I think they dream of small towns, stone walls, beacons of light, seas pounding on rocks, pine trees and maples, sugar shacks, town meetings, country stores, rolling hills, and town greens — all those markers that tell us where we are when we're here. . . .

I wonder how many of us who live here take New England for granted. This is what happened in the '60s and '70s, and even into the '80s, when some of the most cherished and historic houses in various towns and cities in New England fell to wrecking balls. In their place rose condo complexes, parking lots, home developments, and department stores. We forgot how lovely those [historic places] were.

Source: Mel Allen. "Why People Love New England." *New England Today*. Yankee Publishing, May 10, 2017. Web. Accessed May 15, 2017.

What's the Big Idea?

Take a close look at this passage. What comparison is being made between how visitors see New England and how residents view it? What can you tell about Allen's view of New England?

FAST FACTS

- Total Area: 72,000 square miles (186,500 sq km)

- Population: Approximately 14.7 million people

- Largest City: Boston, Massachusetts

- Largest State by Population: Massachusetts

- Smallest State by Population: Vermont

- Largest State by Land Size: Maine

- Smallest State by Land Size: Rhode Island

- Highest Point: Mount Washington, 6,288 feet (1,917 m) above sea level

- Lowest Point: Atlantic Ocean, at sea level

- Name: Rhode Island has the longest name of any state. Its full name is Rhode Island and Providence Plantations.

- Plants: Maine produces approximately 98 percent of the wild blueberries in the United States.

- Money: Crane & Co. in Dalton, Massachusetts, has provided the US government with paper to print money since 1879.

STOP AND
THINK

Tell the Tale

Chapter Two talks about the first European settlers in New England. Imagine you were with the Pilgrims during that first winter. Write a journal entry describing how it feels to be in an unfamiliar landscape.

Why Do I Care?

You might not live in New England. You may not even visit New England soon. Why should you care about deforestation in New England? How are you affected by the logging that happens there?

Say What?

Reading about a new region can mean learning a lot of new vocabulary. Find five words in this book you've never heard before. Use a dictionary to find out what they mean. Write the meanings in your own words. Use each word in a new sentence.

Take a Stand

Chapter Six talks about the different ethnic groups that live in New England. Some families have lived in the United States for many generations. Do you think it is important for them to remember the culture of their homeland? Why or why not?

GLOSSARY

abolish
to do away with something

alliance
a union between people
or nations

blacksmith
a person who shapes
metal by heating it and
then hammering it on an
iron block

buoy
a floating object anchored in
a body of water

commercial
relating to business

ferry
a boat used to move people,
vehicles, or goods

fungus
living things such as molds
and mildews

herbivore
a plant-eating animal

steeple
a church tower

textile
a woven or knit cloth

ONLINE
RESOURCES

To learn more about New England, visit our free resource websites below.

Visit **abdocorelibrary.com** for free Common Core resources for teachers and students, including vetted activities, multimedia, and booklinks, for deeper subject comprehension.

Visit **abdobooklinks.com** for free additional online weblinks for further learning. These links are routinely monitored and updated to provide the most current information available.

LEARN
MORE

Rowan, Hope. *Ten Days in Acadia: A Kids' Hiking Guide to Mount Desert Island*. Yarmouth, ME: Islandport Press, 2017.

INDEX

About the Author

Samantha Bell is the author of more than 50 nonfiction books for children. She lives in the South, but she can't wait to visit New England again. She'll go as a leaf peeper to see the beautiful fall foliage.